Outrageous Fortunes

Up and Down and Around

The Incredible Pierpont Morgan

Samuel Adams's Revolution

The Iron Will of Jefferson Davis

Cass Canfield

OUTRAGEOUS FORTUNES

THE STORY

OF

the Medici,
the Rothschilds,

AND

J. Pierpont Morgan

Harcourt Brace Jovanovich

New York and London

Library of Congress Cataloging in Publication Data
Canfield, Cass, 1897–
Outrageous fortunes.

Bibliography: p.
Includes index.
1. Medici, House of. 2. Rothschild family.
3. Morgan, John Pierpont, 1837–1913.
4. Bankers–Biography. I. Title.
HG172.A2C35   332'.092'2 [B]   80 -24299
ISBN 0-15-170513 -5

Printed in the United States of America

First edition

B C D E

To my grandsons
Temple Emmet Canfield
and
Lewis Cass Canfield

Introduction

B ANKING has a long history. The use of metals in
coinage goes back to the origins of civilization: in ancient
Sparta iron was the medium of exchange, while at one
time the Scots even used nails. The more valuable metals
—lead, copper, silver, and gold—gradually displaced the
cheaper ones. The Hittites in Asia Minor struck the first
silver coins around 1500 B.C.

With the rise of the organized state, coinage became
the special prerogative of the king, although some private
persons also exercised this privilege. Money was of course
necessary for the considerable trade that existed within
Europe and between Europe and the East during the
long period between the rise of Egypt and the Middle
Ages. It was the Phoenicians who established trade routes
throughout the Mediterranean in the pre-Christian world;
they imported spices and perfumes from the East and
carried on trade with East Africa. In the centuries following the birth of Christ the Romans traded extensively
and Rome became the monetary center of the West.

The lending of money goes back to the Phoenicians;
Christian church-regulated pawnshops charging only 3

percent interest were common two thousand years ago. Pawnshops also existed in Greece and Rome.

Wherever there was gold, bankers appeared. Banking was practiced in the ancient temples of Egypt, Babylonia, and India. In Greece, Solon forbade selling men into slavery because they had failed to pay interest. Private banking existed there in 600 B.C., at the same time that King Alyatta of Lydia, father of Croesus, invented gold coins. By the tenth century wealthy monasteries in Greece performed banking functions. During the Middle Ages money lending was practiced mainly by Jews, partly because Hebraic law against charging interest was less binding than the Christian or Mohammedan law, and partly because Jews were generally prohibited from owning and working land.

Pawnshops developed along with banking but they never enjoyed the same prestige, probably because the amounts of their loans were generally small. In the fourteenth century the Bishop of London bequeathed a thousand silver marks to establish a free pawnshop, presumably for the poor; this effort, like similar Italian ones, failed. Consequently, the Vatican permitted pawnshops, called *Sacri monti di pieta*, to charge sufficient interest to offset expenses. By the end of the fifteenth century, monks had established pawnshops throughout Italy; Savonarola started the first one in Florence. From Italy pawnbroking gradually spread over continental Europe —to Augsburg, Amsterdam, and Brussels.

Pawnshops began in England with William the Conqueror in the eleventh century. Three hundred years later Edward III pawned his jewels in order to finance his war with the French.

During the Crusades (1096–1272) commerce between Europe and the Levant increased greatly and banking interests controlled Palestine, Italy, and to some degree France. The cities of Florence, Genoa, Venice, and Pisa flourished; the florin was coined in Florence in 1252; the ducat in Venice a few years later, and in France Saint Louis crowns during the same period.

From the mid-twelfth to the mid-thirteenth century there was great prosperity from Cairo to London. Lively trade made the expansion of currency necessary and, because gold was in short supply, bills of exchange were introduced. Thus an international system of banking was created so that a merchant in Barcelona, in order to finance a shipment of goods, could borrow in his currency, promising to pay in Florentine florins sixty days later. In such transactions the exchange rate was specified at below the actual rate, and the lending bank would make about 10 percent without being subject to any religious prohibition against charging interest. At the end of the thirteenth century the money changers of Venice became bankers, but not until four hundred years later did they use the check.

In northern Europe the Hanseatic League was formed for mutual defense. This association of industrial towns, dating from the thirteenth century, first included seventeen cities and later fifty or sixty, and extended to the borders of Burgundy. The merchants of all these towns bound themselves to trade exclusively at the fairs of Champagne, which the Italians reached over the Alps or by sea through Marseilles.

The world was changing fast. When Vasco da Gama found a sea route to India at the end of the fifteenth century, Italy ceased to dominate Asiatic trade. Antwerp, Genoa, and London then became important centers of commerce. Yet at this time and during the reign of Henry VIII, England could not compete in trade with France since London had but forty to fifty thousand inhabitants as compared with the large population of Paris. Sophisticated techniques of banking were developed in early Renaissance Italy, where city states like Florence, Venice, and Genoa were important trading centers.

The Medici of Florence developed into one of the great banking families of history; their story is as fantastic as the times they lived in.

ACKNOWLEDGMENT

I am grateful to Joan King for editorial assistance
and for help with the illustrations.

Contents

Illustrations

The Medici

THE MEDICI OF FLORENCE were the great Tuscan merchant princes. Their famous emblem, red balls on a field of gold, was originally a pawnbroker's sign. Together with the Bardi, Peruzzi, Strozzi, Albizzi, Donati, and Capponi, they were the earliest European bankers to achieve international importance. One of the reasons for their rise was the rapid expansion of Italian economic life at the time of the Crusades, another, the collection of Papal dues throughout Christendom, which the Italian bankers handled.

The Medici story covers nearly three and a half centuries—from 1400 to 1748. They rose from simple bourgeois bankers and merchants to become the dominant family of Europe; until toward the end of their power a Medici was on the throne of many countries on the Continent. The rise of this banking dynasty is closely tied to the intricate politics of Florence, which it dominated for so long.

In 1400 Florence was a democracy and the most flourishing state in Europe. This was the "morning" of the Renaissance, when a burst of individualism—in con-

trast to the collective spirit of the Middle Ages—swept
over Italy. The people felt confident of themselves and
of their ability to accomplish great things. This creative
energy was first concentrated in Florence, which produced such artistic geniuses as Brunelleschi, Donatello,
and Masaccio. It also produced inspired men of business
like the Medici, who transformed a commercial market
into a capital of the intellect.

At this time, Italy was divided into rival city-states
almost continuously at war with one another. In the
words of Jakob Burckhardt, the nineteenth-century his-
torian of the Italian Renaissance: "A mixture of good
and evil is found in the most remarkable combination in
the various Italian states of the fifteenth century." The
times were unruly; along with the flowering of a human-
istic culture that permeated all classes of society, there
existed among the liberty-loving people a restless urge
to violence.

In this atmosphere it was necessary for the businessmen—the first in Europe to develop merchant banking
into an art—to achieve political power in order to survive. Foremost among them were the early Medici. Of
humble origins, they sided with the workers against the
nobles and succeeded in gaining power without antag-
onizing the artisans and peasants.

It is paradoxical that the touchy, suspicious Florentines
should have tolerated Medici rule, although it was exercised at first with moderation. The early Medici were
diplomatic as well as clever. Their ancestors were farmers
from the Val d'Arno. Their descendants started the
Medici bank through their successful trade in wool,
silk, and alum. In 1304 one of them, a workman named

Giovanni de' Bernadino, started an uprising, invading the wool sector of Florence: his followers pillaged and razed nearly two thousand buildings. Later, Bernadino took part in still another Florentine conspiracy; it failed, and Bernadino was beheaded. Such violence was common at the time, when rival business groups were striving for power.

The death of Bernadino in 1341 and the scattering of his followers gave the Strozzi, one of the leading families of Florence, new prestige and additional business. Andrea Strozzi, the banker, attempted to take control of the city government but was unsuccessful, and Florence seemed to be on the brink of civil war when a coalition of notables, headed by Salvestro de' Medici, took over. There followed an orgy of pillage and brutality.

Salvestro, an outstanding merchant, restored order and succeeded in establishing a democratic government. In 1378 he was elected Gonfaloniere, a position that gave him control of the police. But the period of his rule was brief: new popular uprisings sponsored by the wool carders resulted in his banishment from the city.

When the Florentines decided to call in another Medici to end the disorders, they selected Giovanni di Bicci, a descendant of Salvestro. In 1421, at the age of sixty-one, he was elected Gonfaloniere. Giovanni, who had inherited a fortune, was a wise, discreet businessman; modest and generous, he lacked worldly ambition. He spent vast sums on his city, commissioning Brunelleschi to rebuild the church of San Lorenzo with money donated by himself and seven other leading Florentine families. He was greatly admired for his modesty, his ability as a banker, his expenditures for the public benefit, and his encouragement of the arts.

Moreover, Giovanni won political support by opposing a war against Venice, its object being to arrest the growth of Venetian commerce and finance. This growth had been accelerated by trading privileges acquired by

Giovanni de' Medici

the Venetians from Eastern countries, so that there was danger of the Venetians monopolizing the silk trade, leaving little of it for Florence.

Giovanni was clever not only in helping the workers by his tax reforms, but also in favoring big business and the bankers at a time when they needed support. He could be described as a bourgeois pragmatist and a prudent man—qualities that made the Medici great.

When Giovanni defended the title of the Antipope John XXIII at the Council of Constance (1414), it looked as if he had abandoned all prudence. One wonders what led him to defend and finance a pontiff whose title to the papacy was questioned. True, Giovanni had advanced John considerable sums which he hoped to recoup; also, Giovanni's son Cosimo, who had been sent to Constance, pressed his father to continue his support of John. The Medici appeared at this Council partly because such gatherings in the fifteenth century provided a meeting place for important dignitaries from all parts of Europe. It was like an international business convention today, for there a Medici of Florence might encounter a Fugger banker from Augsburg. The upshot of the Council was that Martin V was chosen Pope. John was thrown into prison and his ransom fixed at 35,000 florins.* Giovanni paid the ransom, and entertained John as his personal guest in Florence.

* The Florentine gold florin dates from 1252; it was the only coin in the subsequent two hundred years to maintain what was for long an internationally accepted stable value. Taking the value of gold at the official rate of $35 an ounce, the florin was worth $4. In interpreting these figures it must be borne in mind that the purchasing power of money in Renaissance Florence was enormously greater than it is today.

Giovanni died in 1429. He was much admired by the people of Florence and left an immense fortune to his sons Cosimo and Lorenzo.

Cosimo was the first to succeed in becoming a strong, unquestioned ruler of Florence, a city that was jealous

Cosimo de' Medici

of her liberty. He ably extended the Medici business, though his interests were also scholarly. His bank maintained branches in Rome, Milan, Geneva, Bruges, Ancona, Pisa, London, and Avignon. His brother Lorenzo, a patron of Renaissance artists, was described as "the perfect flower" of the Medici family.

Cosimo, also a patron of art, encouraged the great artists of his time—Ghiberti, Brunelleschi, Donatello, Fra Angelico, Lippi, and Ucello. In 1444 he founded the Medici Library, the first public one in Europe, sent agents to big European cities to purchase the works of ancient authors for it, and spent vast sums on manuscripts. In addition, he supported the Platonic Academy, where he entertained humanists, scholars, and artists.

A financier of the first rank as well as an able ruler, Cosimo left his son Piero the richest man of his time. Cosimo used his financial power to help his city: in 1452, when Venice and Naples were at war with Florence, he called in the debts from these two enemy states, making it impossible for them to continue fighting. His banking power was so great that he kept Edward IV on the throne of England during the Wars of the Roses by lending him money.

Cosimo increased the family's fortune and its political prestige; helped by his political ascendancy, he absorbed one rival bank after another. He took calculated risks, and was a negotiator rather than a soldier.

For thirty-five years Cosimo ruled by permission of a fickle, excitable mob in a tumultuous period characterized by unrest and intrigue. He took great trouble to find favor with his people, relying on them for protection from the jealous nobles. Realizing the necessity of entertaining the populace, he amused them with frequent festivities and feasts. In addition he financed hospitals, contributed heavily to charities, and built splendid monuments.

Despite his efforts the Albizzi family, enemies of the Medici, stirred up revolt. In 1433 they brought Cosimo to trial before the assembly of the Signoria and he was thrown into prison. For several days he fasted in prison, knowing well that poison was the preferred method of dealing with difficult opponents. At this low ebb of his fortune he persuaded his jailer to put him in touch with the Gonfaloniere, to whom he gave 1,100 florins in return for help to escape to the frontier. It was rumored that Cosimo had traveled to Venice, to set up the headquarters for his bank there. Had he done so, this would have meant a great loss to Florence, since not only had the Medici made their own fortune in Florence, but they had made Florence's fortune as well.

Scarcely a year after his escape, Cosimo was welcomed back by the fickle Florentines. He had left a public enemy, but on his return he was acclaimed with garlands and banners. He announced that he would not punish his enemies, but would work for unity.

Cosimo's talent for getting the support of all classes was evidence of his political genius. He ruled by wealth rather than by force, and used his power to promote social improvement. He maintained good relations with the Orient, whence Florence imported the silk used in Florentine workshops. At the same time, he relieved his people of too much dependence on imported silk by ordering every peasant to plant mulberry bushes.

On his death in 1464, Cosimo was named Pater Patriae for his services to the state. His long, hooked nose was typical of the Medici. His thick ears and coarse lips were not the features of an aristocrat; he remained a man of the people.

Cosimo was succeeded by his son, Piero, nicknamed *il Gottoso*, the gouty one. Although Piero was by no means incompetent, he lacked his father's judgment and got into trouble by calling in loans in order to buy real estate. This action caused distress among rich depositors in the Medici bank like the Pitti, who joined with other important families in forming the Poggia conspiracy, sending bands of thugs into Florence to assassinate Piero. Once again Florence faced civil war, but Piero showed energy and political acumen. By means of gifts, promises, and threats, he persuaded a large contingent of the Poggia party to join his own.

Another crisis for Piero was the outbreak of war in 1467, pitting Florence, Milan, and Naples against Venice and her allies. Actually, it ended comically: the opposing mercenary armies became tired of fighting and fell asleep in their tracks on the battlefield, while the opposing captains visited each other to gossip about the day's events!

Piero died in 1469, leaving two sons, Lorenzo and Giuliano. Lorenzo, called *il Magnifico*, was a poet of considerable distinction; in his house Pico della Mirandola and Politian, famous men of letters as well as the members of the Platonic Academy, were constant habitués. Here, too, Michelangelo began his work as a sculptor.

G. F. Young, author of *The Medici*, has written of *il Magnifico*, "Probably no other man has ever had great talents in so many directions." Although Lorenzo was an autocrat, he managed to retain elements of the democratic process; his rule was unsupported by military

force. He gave grand pageants out of his own pocket
and made his city the artistic and intellectual capital of
Europe. Yet Lorenzo's personal needs remained modest.
He lived in villas, not in princely castles; he was part
of the life of Florence and had the unpretentious air of
the early Medici.

Lorenzo the Magnificent

What made Lorenzo "magnificent"? It was his talent for harmonizing art with life; he combined statesmanship with business sense and love of the arts. Many of the Medici were refined and sophisticated, but they were cunning as well. They took every opportunity to eliminate competitors and to outmaneuver rival banks which they would then buy up cheaply. Lorenzo was a ruthless financier on occasion; he had to be, for the times demanded it.

Florence had become extremely important; her ships were trading in the Black Sea, in Asia Minor, Africa, England, France, and Flanders. In France, Florentines who had been banished from their city became so numerous and powerful that people would speak of Lyons as a French Tuscany.

But Florence had one enemy who would not be subdued—Pope Sixtus IV, who aimed to dominate Italy with his Papal States, whereas Lorenzo took the position that the hope of repulsing foreign invaders lay in the unification of all the nonpapal powers in Italy. Furthermore, Sixtus refused to appoint Lorenzo's brother Giuliano a cardinal. Tension mounted, and in 1478 Sixtus conspired with Francesco Pazzi to murder Lorenzo and Giuliano. On the way to church one day Francesco put his arm around Giuliano's waist to make sure that he was not wearing a coat of mail; then, having reached the church, Francesco split Giuliano's skull, killing him during the consecration of the Host. But the other conspirators failed to kill Lorenzo and he escaped. Meanwhile the Pazzi mob appeared in the Piazza della Signoria to arouse the people, but they, having heard reports of the murder of both the Medici, rose in rage to avenge Giuliano and

Lorenzo. The Pazzi supporters were massacred and their corpses dangled from the windows of houses.

Thwarted, Pope Sixtus excommunicated Florence. Lorenzo not only had to face that problem, but also war against Florence by Sixtus and by Ferrante of Aragon, King of Naples. In fact, at the end of 1479 it looked as if Florence would be invaded. The situation was ominous for Lorenzo, since Ferrante's cunning and brutality were notorious. At this low point Lorenzo took the grave risk of going to Naples to talk with the king. There he remained for several months and during this time persuaded Ferrante, who admired his courage, to abandon Sixtus and join him. Lorenzo's relations with the Vatican were resumed when Sixtus IV died in 1489.

The people of Florence accepted a strict constitution from Lorenzo, whose position of leadership seemed solid —until the monk Savonarola appeared on the scene. In the latter part of the fifteenth century Savonarola achieved what Pope Sixtus and the conspiracies of the nobles had failed to do. His first fiery sermon at San Lorenzo, the Medici church, was delivered in 1483. He denounced the rich and commanded them to abandon their luxuries. Lorenzo, during the nine years of life remaining to him, never attempted violence or intimidation against this monk who threatened him with divine retribution, and invasion by the French as a punishment from God. Moreover, Savonarola was allowed to preach freely. The only recorded meeting between the two antagonists took place at Lorenzo's deathbed in 1492, when Savonarola demanded that the ill man confess his sins and give the people back their liberty. According to the *Chronicle of Florence*, Lorenzo made no reply and turned his face to the wall.

Savonarola

After the death of Lorenzo the reform group, led by Savonarola, grew stronger. Savonarola called for a coup d'état which occurred during the rule of Lorenzo's son, Pietro, a weak character and a bungler. It was unfortunate that Pietro ruled Florence when French armies, urged on by Savonarola, came swarming over the Alps.

Pietro considered himself a great negotiator and made overtures to the French, hoping that they would help his cause, but this tactic failed. Angered that their city should yield without a fight, the Florentines had their Council declare Pietro a felon. His brother, Cardinal Giovanni, attempted to appease the hostile crowd, but had to run for his life. This flight removed the last obstacle to the "Dictatorship of God." Christ was proclaimed King of Florence, and the Florentines cast their jewels and fine clothing onto pyres of vanity.

Savonarola's ascendancy did not last long: Pope Alexander VI excommunicated him soon after for his heretical stand on religious reforms. The Signoria of Florence condemned him and in 1498 he was sentenced to die at the stake.

The burning of Savonarola

The early Medici were more than art patrons; they sought to be the equals of their protégés in so far as that was possible for amateurs. Cosimo and Lorenzo in particular informed themselves about arts and letters. At the Villa Largo the most lively minds of the time attempted to define Humanism, which in the fifteenth century preoccupied Europe's cultivated men. The mainspring of spiritual and intellectual concern had shifted from God to man, to the individual, as opposed to the collective uniformity of the Middle Ages. Savonarola and those he inspired were an exception.

Under Cosimo and Lorenzo the culture of Florence made great strides. The sudden brilliance of Florence in this period resulted from the coincidence of vast opportunities, an exceptional burst of creative talent, and gifted leaders. Yet if the Medici had achieved great power, in the fifteenth century they had only recently acquired high political position. As compared to the established European dynasties, they were considered parvenus.

After Savonarola had been burned at the stake, invasion from abroad still threatened Italy, so Cardinal Giovanni met the principal foreign powers in Mantua to try to work out a peace settlement for the whole peninsula. At this conference Giovanni obtained military backing for the return of the Medici family to Florence. In 1512 five thousand foreign mercenaries entered the city, and further invasion was only averted when their rulers were dissuaded by a payment of 140,000 ducats.

Not only rulers made deals in wartime; their commanders—the condottiere—on occasion did the same.

Mercenaries treated war as just another game of chess.
Unlike today, when wars are waged with the aim of
destroying the foe, Renaissance armies usually stopped
fighting once it became apparent that one side or the
other had the advantage.

Giuliano de' Medici

Giuliano de' Medici became the next ruler of Florence
in 1513. Then thirty-three, he aimed to be a good leader,
declaring himself "a man of the people." However, he
proved himself no more than a tool of Cardinal Giovanni,
who became Pope Leo X in 1513. Leo, anxious to com-

plete the construction of Saint Peter's in Rome, increased the sale of indulgences—a policy that eventually led to the Protestant Reformation.

Giuliano's successor, Pope Clement VII, a cousin of Leo X, was a calculating, withdrawn man. He led a tumultuous life. When Charles V, Emperor of the Holy Roman Empire, attacked the Vatican in 1526, Clement took refuge in the Roman fortress of Castel San Angelo in order to save his life. He was not released until he promised to renounce his claim to Lombardy.

Clement VII was a clever negotiator; he supported Francis I of France, who offered hope of arranging the

Florence in 1500

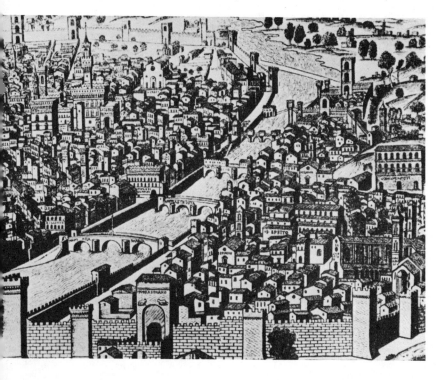

withdrawal of the imperial troops from Italy. The friendship between Pope Clement and Francis paid off handsomely and led to the marriage of the Pope's young cousin, Catherine de' Medici, to the heir to the French crown. But this alliance failed to protect Rome from Charles V, whose army was composed of Lutheran soldiers intent on destroying the Holy City. In 1527, they sacked Rome and Clement again fled to the Castel San Angelo, where he remained for several months. Then a messenger brought news that following a revolt the Medici had been expelled from Florence. Disguised as a peddler, the Pope escaped, returning to a devastated Rome a year later. Florence also was in ruins.

Clement managed to make his peace with Charles V. Together, they laid siege to Florence, which resisted gallantly for ten months. The return of the Medici to their city in 1530 was not a joyful event; the dissolute Alessandro de' Medici was made ruler and abolished the republic. In 1532 he was proclaimed the Duke of Florence by Charles V.

Although a man of outstanding intelligence, Clement was disliked by the Florentines as well as the Romans for his deviousness; upon his death in 1534, bonfires were lit in Florence and Rome to celebrate the event. Nevertheless, Clement made his family so dominant at the time that the political history of Europe became, in considerable part, that of the Medici.

Alessandro's successor, another Cosimo, became Cosimo I and was declared Grand Duke of Tuscany and thus became a European sovereign. An able politician but a harsh administrator, he ruled the largest and most powerful state in sixteenth-century Italy. He supported

Florentine artists but, with the passing of the years, they had become as mediocre as the academies had become pedantic. In addition, he laid out the famous Boboli Gardens, developed the ports of Pisa and Livorno, built roads, and dug canals.

Cosimo I reigned from 1537 to 1574. He reorganized the government of Florence so that, upon his death, it was in the form that it retained until the French Revolution. It was he, with his drive for political power, who was the founder of the Medicean monarchy, rather than his predecessor, Duke Alessandro. With his accession Florence became a different place—a city-state ruled by an absolute sovereign. Although the Florentines lost their

Villa Medici, Florence

liberty, the citizens of the grand duchy of Tuscany enjoyed public order and a security that the republic had never provided. But the magnificent cultural impetus of the fifteenth century was no more, despite the lavish patronage of the ducal Medici; for the art of early Renaissance in Florence had been nourished by the freedom of its citizens.

The history of the monarchical state headed by Cosimo I and his successors is uninspiring. Its rulers, who abandoned banking as beneath their royal dignity, became inept, so that Florentine influence declined; by the first half of the eighteenth century Tuscany had become a pawn on the European chessboard, manipulated by the Great Powers.

And so, after three and a half centuries, the Medici disappeared as rulers of Florence. Despite the serious shortcomings of some members of the family, the early, democratic Medici made an important contribution to European development. By their patronage they helped to bring about one of the most brilliant artistic movements in history; through their business abilities they established banking on an international scale; and by their moderation they maintained a democracy in a period when Europe was semifeudal.

The Medici made a last, magnificent gesture when the Archduchess Anna Maria Ludovica bestowed upon Florence the vast collection of works of art assembled since the day of Giovanni di Bicci. On her death in 1743 she stipulated that the paintings, sculpture, and valuable books should become part of the patrimony of the Grand Duchy of Tuscany. She further stipulated that this inheritance would be valid only if the masterpieces remained in Florence and were made accessible to people from every country. Thus the old Renaissance Florence was assured of remaining one of the world's most important art centers.

The Medici, one of the great banking families of Renaissance Italy who had begun as money changers, were products of their age. What made the Medici stand out was the diversity of their interests; many were truly men of all seasons who developed their talents as the trade of the Italian city-states expanded.

As the later Medici became more and more powerful as rulers, their power as bankers declined. Indeed, the Fuggers, the banking family from Augsburg in southern Germany, had to bail the Medici out of bankruptcy during the sixteenth century. This Catholic family, which carried the title of Counts and Princes of the Holy Roman Empire, did for the countries of central Europe what the Medici had done for Italy.

They started as weavers and merchants. A prolific family, the Fuggers produced many able sons for carrying on a diversified business which, besides banking, included silver and gold mines in Spain and Peru, copper mines in Hungary, a trade in spices and wool, and silk factories throughout the Orient.

Jacob Fugger

Jacob Fugger, born in 1459, became important in European banking shortly after the discovery of America. He was the outstanding member of the family; trained in Italy, he learned the Italian financial system, which had been perfected from the thirteenth century on. He was called Fugger the Rich; his secrets of success were hard work and good judgment. No other banker in history was more active in financing royalty.

Jacob Fugger arranged the transfer of papal taxes and made loans to the Vatican; his most dramatic act was the financing of the election of Charles V as Emperor of the Holy Roman Empire, which involved bribing the electors. When Charles was a guest of the Fuggers, Anton

Fugger felt so honored that he lighted the fire with an Imperial bond for a debt of $30 million due to him.

The Fuggers rose to power at the time the Hanseatic League had started to decline at the end of the fifteenth century, and when Antwerp was beginning to outstrip Venice as a trade and banking center. They came close to ruin when Philip II of Spain, Charles V's successor, declared his country bankrupt after the disaster of the Armada in 1588 and repudiated his debt to the Fuggers, which amounted to several million gold guilders. Philip's excuse was that whatever he did was for the glory of God.

Anton Fugger burning the Imperial bond

Jacob believed in diversification and rarely undertook grandly ambitious ventures. One exception was his nearly successful attempt to acquire a world monopoly of copper, but usually he concentrated on numerous smaller operations. His vast business, which he kept as much as possible within the family, was based in Middle Europe. In 1527 the family's capital amounted to $150 million, ten times that of seventeen years before. By 1546 the Fuggers, then at their height, were worth $375 million; they owned land in Germany, Hungary, and North Africa, coined their own money, and maintained banks in every European capital.

Their golden period ended at the close of the sixteenth century, when precious metals from the New World superseded the European merchants, and state bankruptcies destroyed the capital of European merchants. A further decline came in the seventeenth century with the decline of the Hapsburg dynasty, whose wars the Fuggers financed.

Jacob Fugger was secretive and admonished his heirs: "Just between us, all is silence." His favorite saying was, "The King reigns but the Bank rules!" He left for posterity many fine buildings in Augsburg and a great collection of manuscripts, books, and works of art; he was the first important German collector. His banking activities are still carried on; the Fugger family remains wealthy.

The Rothschilds

CONCORDIA   INTEGRITAS   INDUSTRIA

THE CITY OF FRANKFURT, GERMANY, emerged as a great financial power in the second half of the sixteenth century, as the religious wars were ending and Antwerp and Lyons were declining. Frankfurt markets were the most frequented in Germany. For three hundred years the Jews of Frankfurt were confined to the ghetto—a single dark alley twelve feet wide. It offered adequate space for a hundred and fifty residents, but crammed in three thousand.

In the 1760s the first of the Rothschild family to make a name for himself, Mayer Amschel, came into a small inheritance. Like all Jews, he had to wear a yellow patch on his coat, was obliged to pay a Jew tax whenever he crossed the town river, and when he walked through Frankfurt, was forced to endure the jeers of urchins shouting, "Jew, do your duty," at which he would good-naturedly remove his hat and bow.

Amschel's forebears had lived in a house with a red shield, Rot-Schildt, from which the Rothschild name was derived. When he was ten years old, Amschel had been sent to school to study to be a rabbi. After a few months he became restless; it was the jingle of coins that attracted him. As a youth he sold cloth, tobacco, and wine, and in his spare time collected coins, acquiring a number of valuable ones. A few years later he went to Hanover, where he worked in a bank.

He won the confidence of Prince William of Hesse Hanau, a very rich man, who summoned him to his palace in order to establish the provenance of some old coins. Amschel was kept waiting while the prince was playing chess. Finally, the prince looked up and asked

Prince William and Mayer Amschel

the young man whether he knew the game, upon which Amschel reportedly replied, "Yes, and if Your Highness will kindly make this move, the game will be decided in three moves." It was.

Ambitious to make his fortune, Amschel at twenty-five realized the importance of titles and honors, and successfully applied for one to Prince William. He became crown agent to the prince, although he was unable to write German or speak it properly. He talked in a strange mixture of Yiddish-Deutsch—the dialect of the ghetto. He was the first Jew to have the privilege of displaying a crown agent's sign in his house.

Mayer Amschel married and had five daughters and five sons. It was a close family whose devotion to one another was enhanced by the persecution they had to endure. Amschel, Salomon, Nathan, Carl, and James all enthusiastically joined their father's business, each at the age of twelve. They worked together as a team and laid the foundation of the House of Rothschild. By the 1790s Mayer Amschel had amassed £13,000.

If an important Lancashire cotton manufacturer visiting Frankfurt on business had not annoyed twenty-one-year-old Nathan with his condescending manner, the Rothschilds might never have achieved world prominence. One day in 1798 Nathan said to his father, "I will go to England to show my superiority over this offensive Britisher." He departed forty-eight hours later, arriving in Manchester with a few introductions, £10,000 in cash, and not a word of English. He started there by buying cloth; then, finding three ways to make a profit, he bought wool, had it dyed, and sold the manu-

factured product. Clearly, Nathan was destined to become the family leader; his brothers remained in
Frankfurt.

In 1806 Napoleon seized Hesse Hanau, one of the
small German states, and imposed a blockade of the
European Continent. Prince William had fled to Denmark, having appointed a man named Buderus to care
for his vast fortune. Buderus made Mayer Amschel his
chief banker.

In 1812 Amschel died, leaving all his money to his
sons. He had been a tireless worker—simple, cunning, but
deeply religious. At the time of his death he had no idea
that he had laid the foundation for a world financial
power unparalleled in his age. It took only three generations for his family to achieve this supremacy. In his will
Amschel provided that female Rothschilds who married
outside the family were to be excluded from the
Rothschild business, along with their husbands. He
ruled that key posts were to be held by members of
his immediate family.

Amschel had been instructed in 1809 by Prince William of Hesse Hanau to invest £550,000 in British consols or debentures, considered the safest investment
anywhere. The prince waited three and a half years for
the certificates; he was anxious because he knew the
mails at the time were unreliable, yet he believed that
his order had been promptly carried out.

Actually, Nathan had "borrowed" the money to help
him buy £800,000 of gold held by the East India Company; he knew that the Duke of Wellington needed it
for his subsidies to England's Continental Allies. The

Nathan Rothschild, 1836

next step was difficult: how to deliver the money to the Duke in Portugal in spite of Napoleon's Continental blockade. Using his agents, Nathan got it through France.

In due course he bought the British bonds at ten points below the price agreed upon with the prince, and fulfilled his obligation to him. He made a fortune, not only from the consols but from his delivery of funds to Wellington.

Nathan, now a Londoner and a naturalized Englishman, established N. M. Rothschild & Sons. He acted as Britain's agent for transfers to the Continent, which totaled £30 million between 1812 and 1814. This conception of the first great clearing house in history entitled him to the £1 million he made in commissions. He had achieved the seemingly impossible by arranging for these subsidies without depressing the pound.

At thirty-four Nathan had become the most powerful trader on the London Stock Exchange. The scale of his operations was unprecedented. The brokers would keep a watchful eye on him as he stood by his pillar ("the Rothschild Pillar") on the floor of the Exchange, and observed that he reaped his best harvests in times of disturbances and wars.

At this time London was the banking center of the world. One of the oldest of London's financial institutions today is Lloyd's, the insurance center. This corporation does not subscribe policies; its risks are taken on by the individual underwriting members, each one signing up for a specific sum. Lloyd's was founded by Edward Lloyd, who ran a coffee house in the City of London in the seventeenth century. Another early London firm is Macatta and Goldsmid, bullion brokers, founded in 1684, ten years before the Bank of England. Today representatives of this establishment meet every weekday morning with the Rothschilds and fix the price of gold.

The Bank of England, the first bank of issue, dates from 1694; it owes its origin to the action of King Charles I, who attached deposits of the London merchants and kept them in the Royal Mint. Alarmed, these merchants deposited the money with the goldsmiths, who made loans on it, so that drafts on the goldsmiths were used for paying bills. From this practice the modern check system developed.

The paper currency of the Bank of England was backed by gold. When the metal was in short supply in

The Bank of England, 1860

1757, Lord Clive of India found £600,000 in gold in Bengal, thus alleviating the situation. Clive's action took place at the onset of the Industrial Revolution. The flying shuttle for weaving was speeding up the production of cloth; coal was being used for fuel instead of wood. Then came Watt's steam engine.

The Bank of England maintains its traditions. It is still protected by a detachment of guards grandly attired in uniforms of scarlet and gold, topped off with black busbies. Nearby, at Lloyd's, the doormen wear smart cloaks and top hats.

In sharp contrast to the stability of the Bank of England was the South Sea Company, founded in 1711 by a group of wealthy merchants. The British government granted it a monopoly on English trade with South America and the Pacific Islands, in return for the company's taking over £10 million of the national debt. The South Sea Company was the special pride of the Tory party, which regarded it as the rival of the Whig institution, the Bank of England. In 1718 the king became the governor of the company.

In the following year the South Sea directors made a more ambitious offer to the government: to assume the entire national debt of £51 million in return for further trading concessions. Alarmed by this extravagant proposal, the Bank of England offered the government £5 million for the same privileges, but it was outbid.

The stock of the South Sea Company soared: from 128 1/2 at the beginning of 1719, it reached 1,000 by July, and its directors made fortunes. Then the bubble burst. The extraordinary success of the South Sea Company had produced a crowd of imitators, setting off a wild mania of speculation and its inevitable result—a crash. There followed an investigation by Parliament, which found that the chancellor of the exchequer had been implicated in the South Sea's speculations. He was expelled from the House of Commons and imprisoned.

Another financial disaster, launched almost simultaneously with the South Sea Bubble, was the Mississippi Scheme. In France people went delirious over this venture, originated by a British financier and gambler named John Law. A French government charter granted Law the exclusive trade on the Mississippi River. It looked most promising at the outset, and shares in Law's company skyrocketed. However, as in the case of the South Sea Bubble, the end came soon and bankruptcy ensued.

These two failures, along with others in their wake, brought heavy losses to investors and shook their confidence in the financial system.

The merchant bankers of London were respected everywhere. The earliest of them, the Hambros of Denmark, dated from the seventeenth century; they were followed by the Rothschilds, the Barings, the Schroders, the Lazards, and the Brandts. In 1810 the House of Brown, Shipley came into being.

In 1795 young Alexander Baring was sent on a visit to America, where he speculated successfully in foreign exchange and brought back to London half a million silver dollars. His political and financial careers were brilliant; he served in Parliament from 1806 to 1835 and was chancellor of the exchequer under Wellington. He was also trustee of the National Gallery and collected Rembrandts as well as fine cabinet works of the Dutch school.

Many years before, Richelieu had observed: "There are six great powers in Europe: England, France, Russia, Austria, Prussia, and the Baring Brothers." The Barings concentrated on the United States, the Rothschilds on Europe, the Lazards on the Far East, and the Hambros on Scandinavia.

The Barings were the great bankers of Europe before the Rothschilds became prominent; they financed the American Louisiana Purchase in 1803 for $15 million. A few years later Alexander Baring took a big slice of a French loan which unexpectedly dropped below its issue price; the explanation was a raid by the Rothschilds, who as newcomers had been ignored in the deal. The Rothschilds, after selling these French *rentes*, bought them back and replaced the Barings as the number-one firm. Nevertheless, Benjamin Disraeli said of Alexander Baring: "He was the greatest merchant banker England perhaps ever had."

The Barings got into deep trouble in 1890 over a big Argentine loan—so deep that the chancellor of the exchequer conferred with the governor of the Bank of England about passing the hat around the City. The key man to approach was Nathaniel Rothschild, since he was the banker the others would follow. But whether Nathaniel would forgive the Barings for having excluded the Rothschilds from the great French loan after Waterloo was another matter. Nathaniel had not forgotten this episode; nevertheless, he put up £500,000 to help the Barings and, through his French cousins, persuaded the Bank of France to put in £3 million. A total of £17 million turned the tide.

It was in this crisis that one of the Barings, fearing that his firm would not survive, told a governor of the Bank of England that he had just taken a "drastic" step: to dismiss all his six-foot footmen and substitute shorter men willing to work for smaller wages. This firing of the tall footmen came as close to panic as a London merchant banker could afford, without losing caste.

Nearly all the English merchant bankers started out as merchants. They are still quietly efficient, shun red tape, and complete complicated financial arrangements more expeditiously than the large commercial banks. They discourage small checking accounts and reduce paper work to a minimum, doing much of their business by telephone.

Lunch at an old merchant bank is a pleasant, informal affair; business is not discussed and the talk is about roses and horses, so that a guest seeking a loan is not aware that he is being carefully scrutinized. Whether or not the merchant banker will demand security for a loan depends entirely upon the impression his client makes.

The atmosphere in London differs from that of an American bank where, in place of reserve, everything is open for inspection; or from Swiss banks where a client finds hidden cubicles and discreet offices with well-padded doors. To the London merchant bankers, their Swiss counterparts appear overly literal, dealing mostly in short-term loans and rarely taking a long forward look.

The golden age of the London merchant banker ended with World War I, when "the City" lost its preeminence to Wall Street. These bankers also suffered from Nazi expansion on the Continent, the decline of the British Empire, loss of the China trade, and the dominance of Labour in the British government. Furthermore, government agencies had started to provide the financial assistance to foreign countries previously given by the banks. However, the merchant bankers of London are still powerful; only a few years ago the Hambros financed the Pan American Building in New York—the largest office structure in the world.

Although the merchant bank is considered a peculiarly English institution, nearly all its originators were foreigners: the Rothschilds came from Frankfurt, the Barings from Bremen, the Schroders and Warburgs from Hamburg, the Lazards from Alsace, the Brandts from Saint Petersburg.

British merchant bankers do not believe that a banker should try to be an industrialist. In contrast, the German banks in the nineteenth century became the great entrepreneurs of Europe. They opened up Asia Minor and financed the Berlin to Bagdad railway.

The British have developed banking into a fine art and the City in London is still the most smoothly functioning money market in the world. To show concern there about anything is simply "not done."

Eighty percent of the world's gold is marketed in the City and two-thirds of world ship chartering is done there. On the London Stock Exchange, 9,500 issues are traded.

The merchant bankers looked upon pawnbrokers as an inferior breed, but pawnbroking continued to flourish in both Europe and America. In 1806 Napoleon I made pawnbroking a government monopoly, and Napoleon III regulated it by laws that are still in force. Today the pawnshop in Paris and other French cities is, in effect, a department of the city administration. The same system exists in most of Europe.

In England the Italian Lombards took over from the Jewish pawnbrokers and gave the name to Lombard Street in the City. Although in the Middle Ages the Jew was the almost universal usurer and moneylender, it is now difficult to find a Jewish pawnbroker in Britain. The trade is carefully regulated, as in most countries, and there is a law against "counterfeit" brokers who deal in stolen goods.

In New York City the Provident Loan Society, organized in 1891 by the Charity Organization Society, does a big business in pawnbroking at low interest rates.

In Manchester, Nathan Rothschild had started his career by purchasing cloth; later, when he handled the British subsidies to Continental powers, he managed to remain friendly with Napoleonic France. Nathan thus performed a remarkable juggling act, accomplished in large part through intelligence obtained by couriers, carrier pigeons, and the exchange of information with his brothers.

It was Nathan who first reported Wellington's victory at Waterloo—a major coup. The news was brought by a Rothschild agent who arrived at Ostend on June 19, 1815, with a freshly printed Dutch gazette. At dawn the next day, across the channel at Folkestone, Nathan, having read the account of Wellington's victory, took the train to London. Later that morning he appeared at the Rothschild pillar of the London Exchange, his face pale and drawn. Immediately he started to sell securities and other brokers followed, certain that Napoleon had won at Waterloo. As the price of shares plummeted, Nathan then bought and bought through agents until the British government, which Nathan had informed on his arrival in London, at an agreed-upon time released the glad tidings of Wellington's world-shaking triumph. Nathan made nearly £1 million from his foreknowledge of Waterloo.

Nathan made few mistakes. He did, however, fail to see the future of British railways, a lapse corrected by his brothers Jacob and Salomon on the Continent, who at Nathan's suggestion sponsored the first railroads in France and Russia.

As banker-in-chief for the British government, Nathan was the leader of the Rothschilds after the Napoleonic war; he was then thirty-eight years of age. Next came twenty-three-year-old James in Paris. The three other brothers in Frankfurt—Amschel, Salomon, and Carl—enjoyed less prestige because of the deeply ingrained anti-Semitism in Central Europe. Within a hundred years after the original Mayer had started to lend money, the family fortune amounted to £400 million.

Mayer Amschel's sons were different from their father. When the old man talked about Jewish history and spun yarns, their eyes glazed; but they came alive at *The Wechsel-Stube*, where money was changed. They worked together closely as a team and gained their customers' confidence by the moderation of their charges.

Salomon, Amschel, and Carl Rothschild

Nathan disliked being slighted—as he was when the Bank of England refused to discount a bill drawn in his favor by the Rothschild bank in Frankfurt. Accordingly, he decided to present a five-pound note to the Bank and ask for gold. Within seven hours he had changed £27,000 and his nine clerks had each changed the same amount, or a total of £270,000. At that point the alarmed Governors of the Bank of England met and conveyed their apologies to Nathan.

A tense, sharp character, Nathan was feared on the Exchange. The only person he trusted unreservedly was his wife, Hannah. Yet he helped a number of friendly merchants to whom the banks had refused loans. He thus took considerable risks for the sake of friendship, although he profited from them on balance.

He was a man who made rapid decisions, attributing his good fortune to his resolve to have nothing to do with an unlucky man or an unlucky place. Nathan enjoyed making money, although he had no time to spend it. His aim was to increase the power of his house, and he accomplished this by concentrating his resources suddenly and unexpectedly to launch a carefully chosen undertaking.

It was difficult to put anything over on Nathan, but a broker called Lucas once did. Late one evening Lucas noticed that Nathan's carriage was waiting in front of the Rothschild residence. Suspecting that something important was in the wind, Lucas followed the carriage to Nathan's office and then appeared there, apparently dead drunk, and collapsed on the floor. Nathan and his associates picked him up and lifted him onto a sofa, where Lucas was then privileged to overhear news from Spain about a promising investment opportunity. Finally the inert Lucas was carried out to the street and sent home in a cab, while the others parted with the plan of investing in a certain Spanish stock on the following day. They were too late! Lucas had already made heavy purchases of the stock.

Nathan was a restless, discontented person. He was annoyed by the stream of begging letters from disappointed investors, some of them threatening. In his later years he would go to bed with a loaded pistol under his pillow.

In 1817 Nathan was asked to raise a loan for Prussia of £5 million. At this time the London merchant bankers made few foreign loans, which were mostly financed from Amsterdam. The Prussian loan was followed by others—for France, Britain, Naples, Portugal, Austria. The French government loan in 1818 was especially notable; the Barings and Ouvrard of Paris were favored as the underwriters, or guarantors, of the 270 million francs involved. Negotiations for this loan were held in Aix-la-Chapelle, where the parvenu Rothschilds encountered an assembly of distinguished statesmen. They got nowhere, and were ignored for several weeks until existing French government bonds mysteriously started to decline in price. As the downtrend continued, other securities fell, until a financial crash for all of Europe loomed. The Rothschilds smiled, for their bold tactic of selling to depress the market had paid off; they were called into the meeting to stave off disaster. At last their advice was heeded—the family was asked to handle the loan.

In 1825 a frenzy of speculation took place in England, and loans were made to several Latin American countries. Nathan took little part in these, being involved in the formation of the Alliance Insurance Company, which became the largest concern of its kind in England. Then the South American loans went sour, starting rumors that the Bank of England might have to shut its doors. Nathan thereupon arranged a transfer of gold from France to the London central bank.

The Rothschilds made Frankfurt the most important money center on the Continent, only superseded in Germany in 1870, when Berlin took the lead. More merchant bankers came from Frankfurt than from any other city, and it was there that the international arbitrage business—the exploitation of the difference in quotations on the same stock in various exchanges—started.

By 1819 Frankfurt had become uncomfortable for the Rothschilds and constant threats were made against them. In that year, when a wave of anti-Semitic nationalism swept through the German Confederation, crowds in Frankfurt broke the windows of the Rothschild bank. The Rothschilds remained there, nevertheless.

The Rothschilds wanted—and needed—peace, and they were influential in keeping it. In 1839, when Leopold of

The Rothschild bank in Frankfurt

Belgium wished to take Luxembourg from the Netherlands by force, Salomon preserved peace by arranging a much-needed loan to Leopold, who then agreed to abandon his scheme of conquest.

The family was now moving in the highest social circles throughout Europe, and their financial supremacy was unchallenged from Napoleon's time up to World War I. Mayer built for himself Montmare Towers, said to be grander than royal palaces. This huge English house was filled with fine French furniture, tapestries, Limoges enamels, and Sèvres porcelains. Meanwhile Nathaniel came into possession of the château and vineyards that came to be known as Mouton Rothschild, near Bordeaux.

But none of the family outshone Nathan. When he died in 1836 at the age of fifty-nine, European securities fell. His funeral in London was attended by the Lord Mayor and many of the British nobility and foreign ambassadors. In the same year his son, Lionel, married his cousin Charlotte, the daughter of a Rothschild in Naples. The wedding took place in Frankfurt to please the eighty-three-year-old Gutle, widow of the original Mayer Amschel, who was delighted that of the twelve marriages made by her male descendants, nine were with Rothschild women.

Nathan left four sons—Lionel, Anthony, Mayer and Nathaniel. Lionel took charge of N. M. Rothschild in London, while Antony and Mayer went in for sports and made the Rothschild stable famous. Nathaniel, a paralytic, collected paintings.

Lionel was well fitted to head the London house at the age of twenty-eight. He had been educated at the German University of Göttingen, which J. Pierpont Morgan also attended, and proved an excellent administrator as well as a hard worker. Like his father, Lionel was active in financing state loans.

In 1847 Lionel was elected a member of Parliament, representing the City of London. Unfortunately, he was prevented from enjoying the position, for members were then obliged to swear belief in "the true Christian faith"; Lionel, an orthodox Jew, refused to take the oath and therefore forfeited his seat. Two years thereafter he was re-elected, but it was not until 1858, when elected for the fourth time, that he could take his seat in Parliament without denying his religion.

Lionel, a popular figure in London social life, was often seen with the Prince of Wales. Lionel had a better sense of humor and a more balanced nature than his father. For nearly half a century, until his death in 1879, he successfully ran the Rothschild business in London. His successor was Nathaniel, the first Jew to become a member of the House of Lords.

Aside from the great Nathan, of old Mayer Amschel's sons the youngest, James, became the most famous. He headed the Rothschild bank in Paris and was made a baron. Carl handled the Pope's finances from Italy, Salomon operated in Vienna, and Amschel in Frankfurt.

James started his career in London helping his brother Nathan, until the decision was made in 1817 to establish Rothschild Frères in Paris. Although a conservative financier like his brothers, James lived lavishly. In the Rue

Lafitte his palatial Renaissance house came to be known as "the Versailles of the absolute monarch of the financial world."

Baron James achieved a high position in Paris, as Prince Metternich attested when he wrote to the Austrian ambassador to France: "The House of the Rothschilds plays a much more important part in France than any foreign government, except, perhaps, the English." He went on to observe that money was of first impor-

Mayer Rothschild (son of Nathan), 1871

tance to the French and that the people accepted corruption as a matter of course. James fitted into this picture. He gave bribes and bought influence as was then customary in France.

The withdrawal of certain basic rights by the French ministry in 1830—like freedom of assembly and of the press—had violent repercussions and led to the July Revolution. James was caught off guard when French securities fell sharply. He lost a fortune but remained rich, nevertheless.

In the 1840s James's wealth exceeded that of all the other leading French bankers combined. With a fortune of 600 million francs he was, after the king, the richest man in France. Nevertheless he was tight; when he decided to see the Paris Exhibition of 1855 he went on a Sunday because the entrance fee on that day was lower.

In 1840 he undertook the construction of the Chemins de Fer du Nord railway, which the government would have taken on had not James bribed both members of the Chamber of Deputies and the press. In addition, he constructed railroads in Belgium, although he made more money from speculating in rails than in building them. And yet, while absorbed in business matters, he contributed to the Jews in Damascus at a time when the other wealthy Parisian Jews did nothing.

James survived serious setbacks, as when a brilliant young man named Carpentier, whom he had appointed chief accountant of the Chemins de Fer du Nord, betrayed him. In 1856 Carpentier applied for a short leave of absence. Although he failed to report back on schedule, he raised no suspicion until the workers lined up on

Baron James de Rothschild

pay day, demanding their wages. The safes, in which the money for salaries was kept, could not be opened because Carpentier had left with the keys. Alarmed,

James arrived with a duplicate set of keys and found that the cash assets of the firm—6 million francs—were missing.

Carpentier, with a number of associates, had also stolen stock certificates of the railroad valued at 25 million francs. He escaped capture by going with his mistress to England and taking a steamer from Liverpool. It was a brilliantly executed robbery.

James absorbed the entire loss; no other citizen of France could have done so. And now he was faced with an even more serious threat—this time from Emile Pereire, whom James had put in charge of the Paris-Versailles railroad.

Pereire left James's employ to become a partner of Achille Fould, a noted financier and a railroad rival of the baron. James had been close to the previous monarch, Louis Philippe, but Fould became a favorite of Louis Napoleon, and in 1849, two years before becoming Emperor, Napoleon appointed Fould his minister of finance.

Thereupon Pereire and Fould founded a giant financial concern, a people's bank called the Crédit Mobilier. It started operations in 1852 with 120,000 shares priced at 500 francs. Within twenty-four hours the stock jumped to 1100, and within a week to 1600. Things looked good for Pereire and Fould, who were out to destroy the baron, and bad for James.

At this point a beautiful Spanish woman, Eugénie de Montijo, daughter of an Andalusian grandee, entered the scene. She was a frequent guest at the baron's parties, and gossip had it that Emperor Napoleon III had made an unsuccessful attempt to seduce her. Aware of this, James succeeded in enticing the Emperor to his parties, so that the budding romance between Napoleon III and Eugénie could burst into full flower.

Toward the end of 1852 Napoleon informed his astounded cabinet of his intention to marry the lady. Pereire could not believe that the Emperor would make this mésalliance and organized an anti-Eugénie movement among the French upper crust. This crisis came to a head early in 1853 at the Tuileries Ball, where the Emperor publicly seated Eugénie and her mother in chairs reserved for the prime minister's wife. Eleven days later Napoleon announced that in Eugénie he had "chosen the woman I love and honor."

Napoleon's decision meant that Pereire had suffered a serious setback. Through the Crédit Mobilier, however, Pereire attacked the Rothschilds by buying a quantity of Austrian state bonds, with the object of dominating transportation in Central Europe.

Pereire kept on with his anti-Rothschild campaign, even though Napoleon was becoming increasingly friendly with Baron James. In 1862 the Emperor paid an official visit to Ferrières, James's great new country estate; he was led through Renaissance pavilions hung with works by Van Dyck, Velasquez, and Rubens. Napoleon was royally entertained, and in the park of Ferrières the party killed 1,231 head of game.

The Crédit Mobilier became the financial arm of Napoleon III and a great power on the Continent. Pereire now determined to use it to launch a new bank in Vienna. But when the Hapsburg ministers were informed of this, they revealed that an Austrian concern of the same type was in formation—a people's bank. It was the Kreditanstalt organized by Anselm Rothschild,

Salomon's son Lionel, and Alphonse, the eldest son of Baron James.

The Kreditanstalt made such a handsome offer for the Lombard-Venetian railway tracks that it succeeded in acquiring this valuable property from the Hapsburg government. In addition, these three Rothschild cousins attacked Crédit Mobilier stock on the principal European exchanges, buying the best securities and leaving the speculative ones for Pereire. The tactic paid off when the Crédit Mobilier undertook to finance Maximilian's ill-fated empire in Mexico and other bad gambles.

In 1860 Crédit Mobilier stock declined from its high of 1600 to 800. By the end of 1866 Mobilier stood at 600, and by the fall of the following year at 140. In this period Pereire applied to Napoleon's finance minister, Fould, for the monopoly of the state's credit business. He was turned down, but could not believe that his former friends in the government had deserted him at a crucial moment.

James had finally won his long battle with Pereire. The baron died in 1868 at the age of seventy-six.

While the Paris and London Rothschilds were flourishing, other members of the family were active. Carl, the fourth son of the original Mayer Amschel, was selected to explore business opportunities in Italy, and in 1822 established a branch of the family bank in Naples. Helped by the Rothschild name, Carl achieved astonishingly quick success; he arranged numerous loans for the various Italian states and, a brilliant trader, became master of the exchanges in Italy. As his power grew, Carl was able to stipulate, in connection with a big

Neapolitan loan, that a gifted friend of his, Cavaliere de' Medici, who had been banished to Florence for political reasons, be recalled so that he could become Carl's business associate. In addition, Carl later insisted that, in view of the low state of the city's finances, Cavaliere be appointed Neapolitan minister of finance.

The Rothschild salon in Naples attracted the best of society, due in part to Carl's wife, the Baroness Adalheid, a charming, generous lady who was much admired. But despite Carl's position in Naples, he decided to retire from business there some months before his death in 1855. His three sons concluded that Italy, unsettled by revolutionary movements, had ceased to be a favorable field for Rothschild operations. The Italian bank was closed in 1861, when Garibaldi put an end to the Kingdom of Naples.

Amschel, another of the five brothers of the second generation, took over the Frankfurt bank from the founder. Amschel was a plain man like his father, discontented, with a penetrating intelligence. His friend Bismarck, the Iron Chancellor, said of Amschel, "He is a poor man in his palace. Childless and a widower, deceived by all his people, even his fine Frenchified or Anglicized nephews and nieces, who will inherit his fortune, treat him badly and neglectfully." After Amschel's death in 1855, Frankfurt gradually lost its importance as a financial center. By the end of the century the Frankfurt bank was closed.

For years Austria had refused to do business with the Rothschilds. None of the brothers liked the idea of settling in Vienna, then a snobbish, anti-Semitic, protocol-ridden city. However in 1822, when the Emperor bestowed upon the four brothers the title of baron in recognition for their handling of British subsidies to the Continent during the Napoleonic Wars, the Rothschild bank was established there at last. Prince Metternich, the Austrian chancellor, then asked Salomon to produce a plan for raising the equivalent of £5 million for the Austrian state. It was Nathan who masterminded this operation, but Salomon invented the original and successful plan of raising the money by lottery.

Salomon handled the difficult, vain Metternich with great skill, always giving him credit for thinking of financial plans that Salomon himself had devised. Although he became an Austrian baron, Salomon chose to live in a hotel and remain a citizen of Frankfurt, since as a Jew he could not enjoy the rights of a citizen in Vienna.

Salomon was both successful and popular. In the 1830s he founded the Northern Railway line; in addition, he financed mines in various countries of Europe. For the benefits he had brought to Vienna, the authorities finally called on him and offered Salomon the freedom of the city. After that he was able to live in his own house and become a resident.

His attractive son, Anselm, was a dandy and big spender. He was accepted in the highest circles of anti-Semitic Viennese society. One day, so the story goes, Salomon took a cab generally used by Anselm and, when he paid the fare, the cabby appeared astonished.

"Isn't that the usual fare?" the baron asked.

"Oh yes," the man muttered, "but the young baron

would have given me two or three times as much."

"Indeed," said Salomon. "But, you see, he has a rich father, and I have not."

In the 1870s the Rothschilds reached the peak of their financial power, being recognized as the railroad tycoons of the Continent. They also controlled large quantities of mercury, copper, and nitrates; they had financed Cecil Rhodes's South African diamond empire; and they floated large foreign loans, including one to the United States. They, who had outsmarted Napoleon, now built railroads in Europe and factories in South America, developed oil in the Sahara and water power in Newfoundland, and financed uranium mines. In 1875, when Prime Minister Disraeli anxiously asked them to advance him £4 million to buy the Khedive's share of the Suez Canal at a time when Parliament was not in session and therefore could not authorize a loan, they agreed, lending the money at 3 percent. This action enabled England to acquire sufficient stock in the Canal so that she rather than France, which had also been bidding for the Suez shares, could rule Egypt.

Within the following decade the Rothschilds in France lent money to the Czar in return for an oil concession in Baku which made them competitors of John D. Rockefeller's Standard Oil. In the course of the nineteenth century they amassed the equivalent of over ten billion dollars—more than anyone before or since.

Forty-year-old Nathaniel Mayer headed the triumvirate of English brothers who flourished in the 1880s. "Natty" was the first Lord Rothschild; he belonged to the third generation and his instinct for finance was remarkable, even for a Rothschild. As head of the Alliance Insurance Company of London he refused to insure the *Titanic,* which he considered "too big to float." Nathaniel was a good banker and an equally good host—an observation applying to the whole family, who are famous for having the best cooks, the finest wines, and the greatest race horses.

But it was Baron Edmond, one of the Paris brothers, who became earmarked for posterity. Starting in the 1880s, he devoted his life to financing destitute Jews and encouraging farming in Palestine. Though he opposed Zionism until the end of his life, he paved the way for the state of Israel. For years it was a discouraging venture, for the Jews whom Edmond helped were not exactly dedicated. Jerusalem had been reduced to a tiny enclave of a few hundred people at the time of the Crimean War in the mid-nineteenth century. Despite the difficulties, Baron Edmond donated £6 million to the cause and formed new colonies of Jews; he drained swamps, built houses, and started industries.

In 1894 Captain Dreyfus, a Jewish officer in the French army, was wrongly accused of treason. Among the crowd watching Dreyfus's degradation stood Theodor Herzl of the Vienna *Freie Presse.* Outraged by this new outburst of anti-Semitism, he came out strongly for the restoration of the Jewish state. He felt it was essential to persuade the Rothschilds to adopt his views but found them unsympathetic, since they had proved that Jews could successfully integrate themselves in any country. Even Edmond rejected Herzl, who died in 1904. But ten years later Edmond admitted that Herzl had been right.

Baron Edmond de Rothschild

Ben Gurion, later President of Israel, said of Edmond at the time of World War I that he had been the builder of the Jewish Settlement in the Homeland. In 1914, when Edmond had moved closer to the Zionists, he revisited Palestine. He was amazed: Tel Aviv had become a city and his miserable little colonies had developed into lush gardens; a nation had been created.

When World War I broke out the Rothschilds, like royalty, abandoned family solidarity for a while and were loyal to their countries of adoption. At the end of the war almost nothing remained as it was—but Rothschild solidarity persisted. Baron Louis headed the Viennese bank when peace came. He bought Austrian state securities in an effort to steady the market while Castiglione, Louis's rival, made a temporary fortune selling them short. Things looked dismal for the Austrian Rothschilds when the families in Paris and London came to the rescue, raising the Austrian currency and ruining Castiglione.

The Rothschild family had a passion for collecting, starting with Amschel and his coins in eighteenth-century Frankfurt. Although his sons were engrossed in building up the business, a hundred years later the third generation were famous for their collections of works of art. In fact they developed a whole school of art dealers, including the Duveens, who served them.

Baron Lionel Rothschild assembled fine Dutch and Flemish paintings; his brother Mayer bought Italian Renaissance furniture and Limoges enamels. In Germany Baron Willy put together a great collection of rare books, and the French Edmond Rothschild owned exceptional engravings. The most discriminating of all was Ferdinand in London, who donated to the British Museum a magnificent collection of crystals, enamels, and wood carvings.

During World War II the Nazis seized the most famous Jewish collections in Paris. No one knew their whereabouts until, in the autumn of 1944, James Rorimer of the New York Metropolitan Museum, acting for the U.S. Army, discovered that many works of art had been kept in two Bavarian castles. Subsequently, one of the shipments of these treasures back to France required thirty-six freight cars which contained six thousand objects.

After World War I it looked as if the Rothschild wizardry was over. N. M. Rothschild & Company, though in the front rank of London merchant banks, was no longer the first of firsts. Nevertheless, experts from the bullion market still met every weekday morning in "Mr. Anthony's room" to fix the price of gold. But after World War II Guy de Rothschild rebuilt the bank in Paris with brilliant success. According to him, "The Rothschilds now are bankers who work sixty hours a week."

The Rothschild working tradition is strong. A third-generation employee remarked: "You don't just work an eight-hour day for the partners; you exchange loyalties with them that go to your sons and their sons."

The Rothschild family consisted of very different individuals, but they all shared the ability to adapt themselves to circumstances, and never lost the instinct of acting together as a family unit.

J. Pierpont Morgan

In order to understand the vast financial operations of J. Pierpont Morgan, some information is needed about banking in the United States during the century prior to his emergence as a national figure in the 1880s.

The Bank of North America, established in Philadelphia in 1781, was the earliest U.S. bank. A decade later Congress chartered for twenty years the first Bank of the United States, which acted as the nation's fiscal agent. Initiated by Alexander Hamilton, it was modeled on the Bank of England; it was a private venture, but the government held much of its stock.

The struggle between the Hamiltonian Federalists and the Jeffersonian Democrats—that is, between the urban advocates of centralized government, and the rural advocates of states' rights—raged for many years after the Revolution. This struggle centered upon the issue of a national bank and, as the years passed, upon the person of Nicholas Biddle, a gentle, cultured Philadelphian.

Nicholas Biddle, a student of classics at the University of Pennsylvania, became a lawyer and later served as secretary to the American Legation in London under

Minister James Monroe. As President, Monroe appointed Biddle a government director of the Second Bank of the United States, and in 1823 appointed him president of the bank. Biddle proved able in this position, but committed the fatal error of making the national bank an issue in the national campaign of 1832 when President Andrew Jackson, an opponent of the Bank, was reelected President; the Bank lost its charter in 1836. Allied with the anti-Bank farmers were self-made businessmen who objected to the Bank's policy of curbing credit and currency expansion. During Jackson's second Democratic administration these opponents of the Bank triumphed and made banking free for all.

During the subsequent decades before the Civil War, wildcat banking spread; these banks issued currency recklessly and inflation set in, so that changes in the value of money bestowed affluence on some and hardship on others. The debtor class benefited, as did the government, which could liquidate its debt cheaply. This power of indirect taxation through inflation originated in ancient Rome.

Banks multiplied in this period when America was rapidly building up its manufacturing capacity, thus lessening its dependence on European industry. Like banks anywhere, they required less capital—about one tenth of total assets—than most businesses. Moreover, their interest rates were flexible, depending on the duration of loans and, unfortunately, on such factors as prejudice about certain industries and the race or sex of the borrower.

Savings banks were introduced soon after the commercial ones. They do not create money, and can safely make long-term investments since their liabilities are not subject to call; their depositors must sign a statement to the effect that the bank may delay payments to them for at least thirty days.

In banking there are certain axioms:

The quantity of money in any given community must bear a direct relation to the amount of work done or to the services exchanged.

The value of money depends on the value of credit instruments in circulation.

When a currency is convertible into gold coin, the issuing authority should never have less than 40 percent of its outstanding currency in gold. In theory at least, central banks like the Bank of England must redeem in gold the paper money they issue.*

The balance of debt between countries must be ultimately settled by the passage of gold bullion from the debtor to the creditor nations.

When the balance of payments is unfavorable—that is, when there exists a difference in value between a country's exports and imports, including invisible items like freight charges and interest on foreign investments—and a loss of gold results, the central bank normally raises its rediscount rate—the interest it charges to commercial banks. This makes money dearer and usually makes business decline and prices fall. In this situation fewer bankers borrow from the central bank, the volume of money contracts, and the ratio of gold to currency improves.

* This statement applied to the United States only until 1933, when we abandoned the gold standard.

In 1862 Lincoln reestablished a national banking system and put an end to wildcat banking—but not to economic radicalism. William Jennings Bryan in the 1890s attracted a big following in the Western and Southern states with his bimetalist doctrine of "free silver"—that is, of expanding the money supply by adding silver to gold as a base, at a ratio of 16 to 1. He was narrowly defeated for the Presidency on this issue.

The greatest merchant banker of them all —J. Pierpont Morgan, born in 1837—came from generations of prosperous merchants. His father Junius, an important banker, was invited by a friend of his, George Peabody, to become a partner in the firm of George Peabody & Company of London. So young Pierpont—"Pip," as he was called—was raised and educated mostly in Europe, where he went to the equivalent of high school in Switzerland and took his degree at the University of Göttingen in Germany. There he worked brilliantly under an internationally famous mathematics teacher who urged Pierpont to devote his life to the subject and become his successor.

Although even as a young man Pierpont suffered from *acne rosaca*, which made his nose red and bulbous, he was a gay youth who at school organized a small group that put on grand balls and entertainments.

He was enjoying himself in Vienna when his father wrote him that Alexander Duncan, a friend of his, had an opening in his firm in New York. Duncan, Sherman & Company were well-established bankers maintaining business relations with George Peabody in London. Pierpont soon was acting as George Peabody & Company's American representative.

J. Pierpont Morgan as a youth

In New York Morgan led an agreeable life as a man-about-town. His account books give an idea of his habits and the cost of living in 1857–58: lunch 30 cents; dinner $1; barber 12 cents; opera ticket $8; sleigh ride $13.62. Along with his thrift went godliness—of a sort; the Reverend William S. Rainsford, Morgan's close friend, wrote rather bitingly that Pierpont's faith was like "a precious heirloom—it should be wrapped up in its own napkin—in safe disuse."

Beneath Pierpont's gruff exterior ran a romantic streak. It flared up in his overwhelming love for a young woman named Amelia Sturges. During their engagement she caught a severe cold in her lung, so Morgan married her and took her abroad to the warm climate of Algiers to recuperate. In fact, he abandoned his career to devote himself entirely to keeping Amelia alive, but four months later she died.

Father Junius had strongly objected when his son impulsively gave up his job to marry Amelia and had little confidence in Pierpont at the time. He considered him arrogant, erratic, lacking in talent, with no urge to work and no spark. "What shall I do with him?" he complained to a friend.

Ever after Amelia's death Pierpont kept his impetuousness under control, finding outlets in the pursuit of power and a love of magnificence. As time passed, his spirits were restored. In 1865 he married Frances Louisa Tracy and continued to concentrate on business. Banking called for unusual skill in those days when railroads and industry were developing feverishly, for which massive amounts of capital were required. Unavailable in the United States, it had to be obtained from abroad, mostly from England. Here is where George Peabody & Company—now J. S. Morgan & Company—came in.

The American economy was then handicapped by alternate booms and deep depressions. During the financial panic of 1857 Pierpont was set up independently by

Junius under the name of J. Pierpont Morgan & Company. The chief purpose of the father-son connection was to persuade British bondholders that their fluctuating U.S. investments would have value in the long run. Without the two Morgans, European investment in American railroads and industry would have been insignificant and the great post-Civil War development could not have occurred.

Pierpont prospered and in 1864, at the age of twenty-seven, he reported his personal income as over $53,000—an enormous sum in those days. In his office he installed the first private telegraph line, keeping in close touch with the movements of the Civil War armies. Until well into the twentieth century Morgan & Company's intelligence was equal, if not superior, to that of any government.

Morgan was shrewd but not infallible. There is a story suggestive of his occasional free-and-easy purchasing habits. Two men who owned a steel mill decided, as they were approaching Morgan's office, that it should fetch $5 million. One of them said to the other, "He's rich, why don't we ask for ten?" As they entered the office Morgan addressed them abruptly: "Now, I don't want to hear any talk from you men; I know all about your plant and what it is worth; I haven't time for haggling; I'm going to give you twenty million. Now take it or leave it."

In Morgan's time it was the growth of railroads—more than any other business enterprise—that caught the public's imagination. Since railroads were the key to the country's development, it was inevitable that much of Morgan's energy should be channeled in that direction.

One of the great railroad achievements of the era was the linking up of the Union Pacific with the Central Pacific at Ogden, Utah, in 1869, thus establishing a rail connection from coast to coast.

These were wild days. Jay Gould, a freewheeling Wall Street financier, was deliberately ruining railroads and reorganizing them, unloading their securities on the public and starting over again. A self-made man, a fighter by nature, he was ruthless. His right-hand man was Jim Fisk, a picturesque adventurer, famous in the sporting world and the idol of his gang, known to every policeman and fireman in New York. Fisk would strut the decks of his Fall River steamboats, dressed in the uniform of an admiral, ogling the girls. The business practices of these two men were abhorrent to Morgan and he thoroughly disliked them both.

Already masters of the Erie Railway, Jay Gould and Jim Fisk together launched a bitter struggle for control of the Albany & Susquehanna, a 142-mile railroad connecting Albany and Binghamton, New York, and a vital link between the Pennsylvania coal fields and New England. Its president was a man named Joseph H. Ramsey. Gould started buying stock in the Susquehanna, preparing for the annual election of directors in 1869, from which its president had been excluded by court order. In Ramsey's absence one of the Gould-controlled directors took possession of his office, locked the doors, and forced the treasurer to transfer stock to Gould's nominee.

In August 1869 the local sheriff seized the property; Erie Railway employees were soon running trains at the Albany end of the line, but the Ramsey party was in

possession of Binghamton. Neither side dared to run the
trains through an intervening tunnel where hostile forces
were stationed at each end. The Erie men attacked
and drove the others out, but were routed in turn by
their opponents. Many were badly hurt in this encounter
and Governor John T. Hoffman called out the militia.
The entire countryside was aroused. Roughs and bullies
hired by both parties joined the fray, so that some six
thousand men became involved. The governor then
appointed General Robert L. Banks as executive agent
to manage the railroad; at last it seemed that order had
been restored.

Gould and Fisk were not yet defeated. They were
still confident that they could put in their own board of
directors at the annual meeting. The bitter struggle was
widely publicized, and people watched the outcome of
the stockholders' election as if it were a national sporting
event. One of the most interested observers was Samuel
Sloan, who disliked both Gould and Fisk. Sloan determined to help Ramsey and his associates with advice. He
told them to consult a promising young banker, Pierpont
Morgan. Pierpont was sent for, and after hearing the
saga of the struggle for control of the Albany & Susquehanna, he agreed to try to rescue the railroad, provided
he was given a completely free hand. He bought six
hundred shares of stock, engaged a lawyer, and took a
train upstate to Albany.

The stockholders' meeting started punctually—without
Gould and Fisk; the latter had tried to force his way in
but had been stopped by a "policeman"—a man dressed
up for the occasion by Ramsey and Morgan! Hot and
disheveled, Morgan and Ramsey then entered the office,

locked the door, and held the election; their ticket won, Ramsey and his colleagues remained in office, and Pierpont was elected vice president. He then returned to New York and leased the Albany & Susquehanna to the Delaware & Hudson Canal Company for ninety-nine years on a 7 percent annual basis.

This was Morgan's first venture in railroad control. The happy solution of a tangled and violent situation had come about because two determined men had the nerve to stand up to Fisk and his mob; the result was that a long overdue reform era in railroading was started. Pierpont, by outwitting Fisk and Gould, achieved recognition as a man of decision and courage.

During the next couple of years Pierpont became deeply depressed about his health. He felt perpetually tired, suffered from headaches and fainting spells, and began to think about retiring from business. But his plan ended abruptly when his father took on one of the boldest ventures then known to international finance. The French had just been disastrously defeated in the Franco-Prussian War of 1870 and the revolutionary Paris Commune had come into being. At this juncture Junius Morgan agreed to support the French ministers by floating a $50-million loan to their government. It was a dangerous gamble. For the purpose he organized a group of bankers which he called a "syndicate"—a term that was new at the time. At first the sale of the bonds went poorly and Junius had to take back quite a lot of them at a heavy discount. Things might have gone very badly for him, had French credit not rallied after the war. Junius's judgment was vindicated and his firm won for

Mr. and Mrs. J. P. Morgan

itself in the world of finance a place second only to that
of the Rothschilds. The loan proved essential to the
stabilization of the shaky French political situation.

Having made a deal of such magnitude, Junius wanted
more than ever to have his son in a strong position to
sell European securities for him in the U.S. market. And
here was that son playing with the idea of retirement!
Junius wrote to Pierpont, telling him that he had talked
to a man named Drexel of the important Philadelphia
banking house of Drexel & Company. "It is possible," he
wrote, "that Drexel may want to see you about a certain
matter." A meeting between the two took place in
Drexel's library, and Pierpont was offered an equal part-
nership in the firm. He protested that he was in wretched
health, but Drexel brushed this aside by proposing that
Pierpont take a vacation abroad for one year. On the
evening of July 1, 1871, the firm of Drexel, Morgan &
Company came into being.

Morgan and his wife took a steamer to Liverpool and
spent some time with the senior Morgans at 13 Princes
Gate in London, a pleasant, commodious house overlook-
ing Hyde Park. From London Pierpont and his wife
went to Carlsbad and the Austrian Tyrol. By that time
Pierpont had regained his buoyant spirits and was able
to take long walks in the mountains. On his return to the
hotel he would settle into a comfortable chair and try
smoking an Austrian meerschaum pipe; but after several
attempts he would throw it out the window and go back
to his innumerable large black cigars, the only form of
tobacco he enjoyed.

The Morgans returned to New York for Christmas.
Pierpont was glad to be back, for he loved America—yet

had no real belief in democracy. He was really British in temperament. He took not the slightest interest in what came to be called café society and shunned any kind of publicity.

J. P. Morgan in his office

The year 1878 at the office had closed well. In those days banking involved long hours, for stenographers were almost unknown. On New Year's Eve Pierpont stayed there very late—until 6:00 A.M.—to close the books. Though he took long vacations, he was a hard worker. In addition, he often had to go to bed for a couple of days to get over one of his frequent headaches. The eruption on his nose bothered him, but he was able to comment humorously about it: "It would be impossible for me to appear on the streets without it." On another occasion he remarked that his nose was "part of the American business structure."

Morgan never claimed to know much about real estate, and as an investment it failed to interest him. Nevertheless, he owned houses in New York and London, a camp in the Adirondacks, and a fishing box in Newport. In 1882, having met Thomas A. Edison the year before, Morgan had his newly purchased house on Madison Avenue provided with an electric lighting system—the first private residence in the country to be so illuminated throughout.

Morgan became involved in railroads on a really big scale when William H. Vanderbilt called on him for help. Vanderbilt had greatly extended the railroad properties he had inherited from his father Cornelius, so that by 1879 he owned three-quarters of the New York Central stock and controlled many of its affiliated and connecting lines. He was a law unto himself: it was he who reportedly said, "The public be damned!" His impulse was to grab, whereas Morgan's was to rule.

Things were becoming ominous for Vanderbilt. The people of New York State objected to having their main railroad controlled by one man. At this point Drexel, Morgan & Company relieved the situation by buying 350,000 shares of Central for distribution to British and American investors, and Morgan became a director of the firm.

During the Panic of 1893 Lincoln Steffens, a famous reporter, was assigned to interview a number of private bankers and observed that of these, "J. P. Morgan was the greatest." Steffens wrote in his autobiography:

Somebody stopped me as I was going out through the bank and laughingly asked me what had happened. "Nothing," I said; "he didn't even see me." "You're lucky," was the chuckling answer. "You have to call him to wake him up. If you had said, 'Mr. Morgan,' he would have come to. And then—" "What would have happened then?" I asked. "Oh," the partner said, "then you would have seen—an explosion." I believed that; it was generally believed on the Street that J. P. Morgan was a dangerous man to talk to. I know that I came to feel, myself, what others on Wall Street felt—a vague awe of the man.

But I went through that awful circle once. . . . My paper had received . . . a typewritten statement from Morgan and Company; it was some announcement about a matter of bonds that had been news for months, and the city editor called me in to read it with him. He could not make it out. It was a long, complicated statement all in one sentence, and I could not read it either. "Take it down to Mr. Morgan and ask him to read it" [my boss] said, and I remember I was startled. I asked . . . if he knew what he was asking of me: to go and put a question to the old man himself. "Yes . . . but it has to be done." I picked up the statement, ran down to the bank, conning the sentence, and ready for the explosion . . . walked into Morgan's office and right up to his desk. He saw me this time; he threw himself back in his chair so hard that I thought he would tip over. "Mr. Morgan," I said as brave as I was afraid, "what does this statement mean?" and I threw the paper down before him. "Mean!" he exclaimed. His eyes glared, his great red nose seemed to me to flash and darken, flash and darken. Then he roared, "Mean! It means what it says. I wrote it myself, and it says what I mean." "It doesn't say anything—straight," I blazed. He sat back there, flashing and rumbling; then he clutched the arms of his chair, and I thought he was going to leap at me. I was so scared that I defied him. "Oh come now, Mr. Morgan . . . you may know a lot about figures and finance, but I'm a reporter, and I know as much as you do about English. And that statement isn't English." That was the way to treat him, I was told afterward. And it was in that case. He glared at me a moment more, the fire went out of his face, and he leaned forward over the bit of paper and said very meekly, "What's the matter with it?" I said I thought it would be clearer in two sentences instead of one and I read it aloud so, with a few other verbal changes. "Yes," he agreed, "that is better. You fix it."

Morgan's behavior as chief vestryman of Saint George's Episcopal Church provides another example of his dominating character. Against the majority of the vestrymen, he insisted upon keeping down their number, saying that he wanted only gentlemen in that body—men he would enjoy having in his home. When his proposal was voted down, he walked out of the meeting.

But Morgan combined humility with arrogance. In London he became so annoyed at his employees who, in the class-conscious British fashion, bowed to him, that he ordered them to desist on pain of dismissal. Yet he had to have his way. When he could not get a friend of his into the Union Club in New York, he proceeded to build his own, the Metropolitan Club.

Morgan spent much of his time on his ocean-going steam yacht, *Corsair*, where he entertained and held important business conferences. Though he was in relatively good physical condition, the eruption on his nose and face continued to trouble him, and he did not get the physical exercise he needed—his horseback rides and long walks were things of the past. In winter the lack of open-air life probably accounted for his frequent headaches and heavy colds but, despite his bouts of exhaustion and spells of illness, Morgan enjoyed life. He had a number of intimate friends—women as well as men. His male friends were members of the Corsair Club, which he had organized. He delighted in feminine society, particularly when his lady companions were pretty and gay. From his yacht trips to eastern Mediterranean ports, he would bring back from the bazaars trayfuls of jewels and knicknacks which he distributed

J. P. Morgan and friend   *J. P. Morgan and Sir Thomas Lipton*

among them. One of his favorites was Maxine Elliott,
a great beauty of the theater.

This playful side of Morgan was perceived by very
few, for he was discretion itself. When an associate,
whom he had called on the carpet for some action, protested that he was only doing what Morgan himself had
been doing "behind closed doors," Morgan replied,
"That, sir, is what doors are for."

Morgan was now at the apex of his career and had
become the acknowledged leader on Wall Street. He
was concerned with most of the important industries in
the country, so it was natural that he should turn his
attention to steel, which had superseded other metals for
construction. The rapid development of the steel industry in the United States attracted world attention.
Andrew Carnegie had come to dominate this field, and
it was his ruthless ambition to control the world market.
At the head of Carnegie's company was young Charles
M. Schwab.

Quite possibly the rapid growth of Standard Oil from
a number of smaller concerns sparked in many alert
minds the project of a similar merger of steel interests.
Whoever the originator, it was Schwab who first advanced this idea with a conviction no other American
industrialist could match. In 1901 Morgan, fired by
Schwab's vision, organized the United States Steel Corporation, the most important enterprise he had ever
undertaken; its capitalization of $1,400,000,000 made it
the largest American corporation yet organized. Morgan
had eliminated Carnegie from big steel; Carnegie decided
to sell out.

After he and Pierpont had agreed upon $225,639,000 as the price for his steel interests, Carnegie asked the financier whether he would have paid $100 million more, had Carnegie demanded it. Morgan replied, "If you had asked, I should have paid it." The initial arrangement was quite informal—a penciled memorandum on a scrap of paper. In due course a suitable document was prepared and signed by both parties.

In railroads, Morgan and E. H. Harriman, a famous financier, were the two great antagonists. One of their struggles involved control of the Burlington & Quincy, an essential line in the important transportation network west of the Missouri River. James J. Hill, another big railroad operator, and Morgan wanted this railroad because it would give the Northern Pacific an entry into Chicago; Harriman had to have it because the Burlington was a competitor in his Union Pacific territory.

Harriman lost the fight for control of the Burlington, and the Morgan-Hill forces breathed a heavy sigh of relief, unaware of the fact that, at that very moment, Harriman was buying up the stock of the Northern Pacific, which now owned the Burlington line. In the course of this fight the Northern Pacific stock soared from 112 to 1000 on the market.

In the Panic of 1907 Morgan, aged seventy, faced and overcame his supreme test. In this emergency people turned to Morgan because he had saved the country in 1895, during Cleveland's administration, when gold resources had been nearly exhausted and the government had been powerless to deal with the situation.

On October 22, 1907, a run on the Knickerbocker Trust Company, a large bank, caused it to fail. As Morgan drove downtown in his brougham, cabbies and policemen recognized him and shouted: "There goes the Big Chief!" On October 24 the president of the New York Stock Exchange, alarmed by the abrupt fall in prices, phoned Mr. Morgan and said: "We will have to close the Exchange." But the "big chief" snapped back, "It must not close one moment before three o'clock, today!" He then summoned the presidents of all the national banks and raised $25 million in a few minutes.

Late on Saturday, November 2, the panic reached its climax. Once again Morgan received the bank presidents in his house. Everyone was at the end of his tether; the bankers' pockets were empty and they saw no way of putting up another $25 million to save the situation. Then Morgan entered the room. With his imposing bulk and his swollen, vivid nose, he was overpowering. Photographer Edward Steichen observed: "Meeting his black eyes was like confronting the headlights of an express train bearing down on you."

Morgan had with him a document stipulating that each trust company, according to its resources, would put up its share of the financial support required.

"There you are, gentlemen," he said.

No one stepped forward. Morgan placed his hand on the shoulder of Edward King, leader of the group.

"There is the place, King, and here is the pen."

King signed, they all signed; it was five o'clock in the morning—Morgan had carried the day. To the extent that one man could function as a central banking system,

Morgan had done it—by the power of his personality rather than through his financial resources.

The next day $13 million did the trick, though one Morgan partner remarked: "There was not a ray of hope in the situation."

Night after night the bankers met to confer in the library in Morgan's house on Thirty-sixth Street. Morgan would sit playing solitaire in the West Room while the exotic and glamorous Belle Greene, his devoted librarian, carried messages from one room to the other. More than once during the long sessions, which lasted until midnight, a plan would be presented to Morgan. He would look up, listen attentively—then shake his head, saying, "No, that will not work," and return to his cards. Eventually, a suggestion for issuing Clearing House certificates was proposed. Morgan did not like the idea but said, "This will work," and approved it.

At last the dreadful week neared its end. Even President Theodore Roosevelt, the decrier of "malefactors of great wealth" (of whom Morgan had once remarked, when Roosevelt was in Africa shooting game, "I hope the first lion he meets does his duty"), issued a statement about Morgan and his associates, praising "those influential and splendid businessmen who have acted with such wisdom and public spirit."

After the exhausting experience of 1907, Morgan gradually retired from business. He was often to be seen in his suite at some great European hotel, seated at a card table and reaching for a silver box containing two packs of cards. He dressed formally with a wing collar, Ascot tie, and white waistcoat; beside him sat Chun, his Pekinese dog.

Morgan, a tycoon of his period, thought of industry not in terms of its thousands of workers—of human beings—but in terms of the investors who supported it and of the directors whose duty it was to protect and enrich the investors. For those directors his standards were high: they must be honest and preferably gentlemen. In fact, he would have liked to see the United States run by gentlemen, and it did not occur to him that these gentlemen might be insulated from their fellow men and run things in a way most comfortable to themselves. After all, he would observe, the politicians liked to run things to their advantage. So, although loyal to his country and its government, his ideas were elitist, as was his conduct of life. The concept of democracy eluded him.

However it is only fair to mention that, in a depressed period at the turn of the century, Morgan put up the money to save the old publishing firm of Harper & Brothers, because he believed that its failure would impoverish many writers and be harmful to American letters. This action cost him $2 million. A decade later, when he learned from his partners that two banks with thirty thousand depositors in a run-down Manhattan district might have to close their doors, he said to them: "Some way must be found to help these poor people. You say that the total risk is only six million?" He accepted the risk of backing these banks and actually lost only $200,000 on this generous venture.

During the Pujo Committee's Senate investigation into monopolies in 1912, Samuel Untermyer, the committee's counsel, questioned Morgan relentlessly about

J. P. Morgan before the Senate

his overriding influence in national finance. The Morgan interests held 118 directorships in 34 banks or trust companies; 30 directorships in 10 insurance companies; 105 directorships in 32 transportation companies; 63 directorships in 24 producing and trading corporations; and 25 directorships in 12 public utility corporations, making a total of 341 directorships in 112 corporations. The combined corporations had resources of over $22 billion, and of the 341 directorships, Morgan's partners held 72. At the close of its report the Pujo Committee said, "The acts of this inner group . . . have . . . been more destructive of competition than anything accomplished by the trusts."

Questioned about his alleged control of the banks, Morgan insisted that the presence of Morgan partners on the boards of other banking institutions did not mean control, that the influence which men exercised depended not on diagrams of "control" but upon their personal stature. Untermyer had asked him: "Is not commercial credit based primarily on money or property?" "No, sir," answered Morgan, "the first thing is character." "Before money or property?" "Before anything else. Money cannot buy it . . . because a man I do not trust

West Room of the Morgan Library

The Morgan Library

could not get money from me on all the bonds in Christendom." Morgan was an excellent judge of men; the quality of his partners is evidence of this—men like Thomas W. Lamont and Henry P. Davison, who were recognized as brilliant bankers.

While other New York millionaires built themselves ostentatious replicas of French châteaux or Renaissance palazzi, Morgan was content to live in his comfortable, inconspicuous Murray Hill brownstone in New York. He set his own style and when, at a late age, he started seriously to build up his vast art collection, he did so with princely assurance. Actually, he was a born collector; as a boy he had treasured bits of colored glass picked up around European cathedrals. Yet many art dealers, disappointed because Morgan did not buy their wares, called him just a vulgar wholesaler.

His serious collecting dated from the 1890s, when he started buying rare books and manuscripts for his library at Thirty-sixth Street in New York. The library, now considered one of the finest in the world, contains such items as a Gutenberg Bible on vellum and the original manuscript of Keats' *Endymion.*

Morgan then turned his attention to works of art and artifacts of every kind—from tiny snuff boxes to large, magnificent tapestries. His taste was traditional; modern paintings had no place in his collection. Nevertheless, his eye for art was remarkable. When a dealer, George Hellman, brought him a small Vermeer painting, Morgan asked, "Who's Vermeer?"—not really surprising because, at the time, there were only four paintings by this artist in the United States. Morgan carefully examined the picture and after a few moments paid $100,000 for it. He seldom consulted experts and rarely made a mistake.

When Morgan had acquired the best in any field, he would quit and turn to something else. His sister once said to him in Naples: "Pierpont, aren't you going to see a dealer in Greek antiquities?" He replied: "I have done with Greek antiquities; I am at the Egyptian." His active mind moved from one interest to another. In his huge collection were the best miniatures, the finest English portraits and landscapes, the richest porcelains, bronzes, and Limoges enamels.

He had an eye for both quality and value. In the 1890s young Joseph Duveen showed Morgan a collection of thirty miniatures, among which six were rare and the rest undistinguished. Morgan glanced at them, asking the price for the lot. When Duveen named a figure Morgan put the six best in his pocket, figured one-fifth of the asking price, and announced what his purchase had cost.

At Morgan's death his works of art and books were

valued by the *Times* of London at $60 million—half his total fortune. The Metropolitan Museum was the largest beneficiary of this collection, one of the greatest in modern times. It was comparable to that of Lorenzo de' Medici's, except that Lorenzo supported his contemporaries whereas Morgan confined his collecting to works of art created before the Impressionists.

In later life Morgan would spend half the year abroad, accompanied by a retinue of servants, art experts, relatives, and usually a charming female companion. These people helped to insulate him from the army of dealers, impoverished aristocrats, and confidence men who laid siege to his hotel.

J. P. Morgan in Rome

Early in 1913 Morgan, accompanied by his daughter
Louisa and her husband, Herbert Satterlee, went to
Egypt. On their way back to New York, the party got
only as far as Rome, for Morgan's health was failing. In
Rome he summoned enough strength to attend an Easter
service, but thereafter lost ground fast. His mind went
back to early days in Hartford and school in Switzerland. The last words his son-in-law heard him say were,
"I've got to go up the hill." Later that same day—March
31, 1913—aged not quite seventy-six, Morgan died. His
body was taken back to New York, where a great
funeral was held at Saint George's Church.

He was an expansive character. Anne Morrow Lind-
bergh describes supper aboard his yacht, the *Corsair*:
"We were transported very swiftly in a closed-in motor
boat to the great steamer. . . . We stepped out onto the
steps and at the top stood Mr. Morgan—great, gruff, cor-
dial, always with his 'superb' manner, large smile, large
gestures, large, hearty 'How do you do'—his round, very
full voice, English accent."

What legacy did Pierpont Morgan leave behind, besides
his art collection, his fortune, and the great enterprises he
established? What he essentially left for American posterity was a tradition of uncompromising honesty. The
last of the American financial Titans, he was a man who
knew what he wanted and got it.

After the death of Pierpont Morgan the character of
American banking underwent big changes. As the years
passed, the corporate image took the place of dominating
personalities like Morgan's and the Federal Reserve System, established by Woodrow Wilson in 1913, took over

the functions of a central bank. And whereas the Morgan firm raised the money to finance the Allies in World War I, the U.S. government took over this role in World War II.

The Federal Reserve Banks adopt their own policies, independent of the government. There are now twelve Federal Reserve Banks with headquarters in Washington, D.C. By fixing the rediscount rate (i.e. the rate of interest on loans to banks), they can control the amount of outstanding currency.

The entry fee into the Federal Reserve System for commercial banks is 6 percent of their capital. Being part of the system has distinct advantages: to a member bank the Federal Reserve will supply currency on demand; the opportunity, in case of dire need, to borrow at a reasonable rate; and a management consulting service. However, only one-tenth of chartered state banks—the larger ones—are members. Joining the Federal Reserve system automatically conveys membership in the Federal Deposit Insurance Corporation, for which banks outside the system are also free to make application.

In the 1920s the United States went through a postwar boom: gambling in stocks was like playing a roulette wheel where the winning number always appeared. The boom lasted for years, so that almost no one could see the end of it. Economist Irving Fisher announced on October 17, 1929, that stock prices had reached "what looks like a permanently high plateau." Meanwhile Charles E. Mitchell, chairman of the great National City Bank of New York, was continuously radiating sunshine. Equally optimistic was the opinion expressed in the Boston News Bureau's "Broad Street Gossip," that "business is now too big and diversified, and the country too rich, to be influenced by stock market fluctuations."

What halted the progress of American business was that businessmen had become bemused with paper values which bore little relation to the production of goods. Various devices were used to stimulate stock prices: company mergers that gave insiders big profits; the piling up of holding companies, with the result that resources at the base of the pyramid would be drawn off by the owners of the concern at the top; and the formation by banks of "security affiliates" which used the depositors' funds to make investments.

Such devices knit spurious speculative values into the economic fabric to such a point that, if values fell, banks and companies would be very hard hit.

The big Bull Market started in 1926 and reached a climax in September 1929; a million people were in the market buying on margin—from housewives to elevator boys. Stock prices, according to Standard Statistics, had more than doubled between 1926 and 1929. A few wise men like Andrew Mellon issued warnings, but there was no one to stop the dizzy spiral. The Federal Reserve tried by means of banking regulations, as did the Morgan firm, almost alone among the bankers.

The boom had seemed permanent although in 1929 wealth was obviously ill-distributed; only 10 percent of Americans enjoyed incomes of more than $5,000, while 71 percent had incomes of less than $2,500 and 19 percent realized less than $1,000 a year—about half the amount necessary for buying bare necessities for a family.

Within a few weeks after October 1929, $30 billion of the value of securities vanished and the legend of Wall Street leadership had been punctured. On the day Franklin D. Roosevelt entered the White House in 1933, the American banking system came to a complete halt.

It had been a collapse beyond imagination. In the middle of 1932 American industry was operating at half of what it had been in 1929; the amount of wages paid out was 60 percent less than in 1929, and business as a whole was running a loss of $5 billion a year. As for stocks, General Motors had dropped from 72 to a low of 7⅝, RCA from 101 to 2½, and U.S. Steel from 261 to 21. The number of unemployed was twelve million.

Yet the Great Depression brought to the United States nothing approaching a political revolution, though it did result in the rewriting of many financial laws. Government action forced a break between banks and the securities business, circumscribed pool operations in stocks, set up a federal agency to police the Stock Exchange, and dismantled illogical holding companies.

To bring the country out of the Depression, Roosevelt stimulated employment by building dams, highways, and playgrounds on a massive scale. He gave the green light to organized labor, so that by 1940 the number of union members had increased to 9 million—three times the number in 1933. In this way, purchasing power became better distributed.

Business activity and prices started to rise when Franklin D. Roosevelt assumed the Presidency in 1933 and inaugurated New Deal hit-or-miss deficit financing, but recovery was a slow process. In August 1939 ten million workers still had no jobs. In fact relief did not come until the outbreak of World War II, when industrial production rose by 25 percent as a result of the massive U.S. military program.

Franklin D. Roosevelt's policies marked a milestone in the banking world; the United States abandoned the gold standard and devalued the dollar. Prior to that, paper currency and bonds were exchangeable for gold. The Baltimore & Ohio Railroad's bonds, issued in 1930, were an example; not only their principal but their interest was redeemable in gold. In fact a gold clause, instituted early in this century, was a routine provision in sales and debt contracts.

It was also in 1933 that merchant banking, in the sense of commercial banks offering securities for sale, came to an end. The Glass-Steagall Bill stipulates that a financial institution must choose between making loans—sometimes long-term—to customers, and underwriting issues of stocks or bonds. The reason for this mandatory separation of functions is that underwriting is a riskier business than making ordinary loans. An underwriting concern may not succeed in selling the total of a security it offers to the public, and so can be left holding the remainder, which is just as likely to go down as up in value.

In recent years the computer has revolutionized banking, speeding up bookkeeping, providing data previously unavailable, and saving money by reducing personnel. Banking has become institutionalized, and the corporate image has taken the place of dominating personalities.

The colorful days of the Medici, the Rothschilds, and J. Pierpont Morgan belong to the past. These great bankers operated in quite different ways; for example, many of the Rothschilds made large sums from playing the market, whereas Morgan never speculated. On the other hand, they all had a number of things in common:

They were lucky—which is to say that they took full advantage of their opportunities.

Their methods were unconventional and often unexpected, but perfectly adapted to the conditions they encountered.

They operated at the right time in the right place.

They wanted power as well as money.

They maintained superb intelligence services and so knew more than their competitors.

They were great collectors of art both by inclination and because fine works of art are a good investment.

They charged fairly for their services.

They were men of their word.

Bibliography

Adams, Brooks. *Law of Civilization and Decay.* 1896.

Allen, F. L. *The Big Change.* New York: Harper & Brothers, 1952.

Balla, Ignatius. *The Romance of the Rothschilds.* New York: G. P. Putnam's Sons, 1913.

Biddle, Nicholas. *Correspondence.* Boston: Houghton Mifflin & Co., 1919.

Brion, Marcel. *The Medici: A Great Florentine Family.* New York: Crown Publishers, 1969.

Brooks, John. *Once in Golconda.* New York: Harper & Row, 1969.

Brown, J. C. *A Hundred Years of Merchant Banking.* Privately printed, 1909.

Canfield, Cass. *The Incredible Pierpont Morgan.* New York: Harper & Row, 1974.

Corti, E. C. *The Rise of the House of Rothschild.* New York: Cosmopolitan Book Corp., 1928.

Cowles, Virginia. *The Rothschilds.* New York: Alfred A. Knopf, 1973.

Dewey, D. R. *Financial History of the United States.* London: Longmans Green & Co., 1909.

Ehrenberg, Richard. *Capital and Finance in the Age of the Renaissance.* New York: Harcourt, Brace & Co., 1928.

Garraty, John A. *The American Nation.* New York: Harper & Row, 1960.

Goddard, T. H. *A General History of the Most Prominent Banks in Europe.* New York, 1831.

Hahn, Emily. *A Book of Gold.* New York: Harper & Row, 1980.

Hammond, Bray. *Banks and Politics in America.* Princeton: Princeton University Press, 1957.

Hidy, R. W. *The House of Baring.* New York: Russell & Russell, 1949.

Keynes, J. M. *Monetary Reform.* New York: Harcourt, Brace & Co., 1934.

King, W. S. C. *History of the London Discount Market.* London: George Routledge & Sons, 1936.

Lane, F. C. *Venice: A Maritime Republic.* Baltimore: Johns Hopkins University Press, 1973.

Mackay, C. *Extraordinary Popular Delusions.* New York: Noonday Press, 1932.

Mayer, Martin. *The Bankers.* New York: Weybright & Talley, 1974.

Morton, F. *The Rothschilds: A Family Portrait.* New York: Atheneum, 1961.

Nicolson, Harold. *Congress of Vienna.* New York: Harcourt, Brace & Co., 1946.

Oliphant, Mrs. *The Makers of Venice.* London, 1887.

Origo, Iris. *The Merchant of Prato.* London: Jonathan Cape, 1957.

Roscoe, William. *Illustrations of the Life of Lorenzo de Medici.* London, 1822.

Rostostzeff, M. *The Social and Economic History of the Hellenistic World.* 3 vols. Oxford: Clarendon Press, 1941.

The Social and Economic History of the Roman Empire. 2 vols. Oxford: Clarendon Press, 1926.

Sheldon, Anna R. *The Medici Balls.* New York: Charterhouse Press, 1904.

Smeaton, O. *The Medici and the Italian Renaissance.* New York: Charles Scribner & Son, 1901.

Strieder, J. *Jacob Fugger, the Rich.* New York: Adelphi Co., 1931.

Tawney, Richard H. *Religion and the Rise of Capitalism.* Massachusetts: Peter Smith, 1962.

Thomas, Hugh. *A History of the World.* New York: Harper & Row, 1979.

Walker, Francis A. *Money.* New York, 1878.

Warburg, J. P. *The Money Muddle.* New York: Knopf, 1934.

Wechsberg, J. *The Merchant Bankers.* Boston: Little Brown & Co., 1966.

White, W. L. *Bernard Baruch.* New York: Harcourt, Brace & Co., 1950.

Young, G. F. *The Medici.* 2 vols. New York: E. P. Dutton & Co., 1923.

Index